MAKE LEARNING AN
INNOVATION

The Smart Way To Crack NEET through Biology and Step Into White Coat

By

COACH RACHITHA

FOREWORD

"Make Learning an Innovation" by Rachitha S N is a groundbreaking resource for NEET aspirants. This book offers a unique approach to master complex concepts and helps to score full marks in the NEET examination.

Expert Guidance

Rachitha's expertise and experience in guiding students have culminated in this comprehensive guide. The book provides:

- Innovative learning strategies

- Conceptual clarity

- Practice questions and exercises

- Tips for effective time management

A Valuable Resource

I am confident that "Make Learning an Innovation" will become an indispensable companion for NEET aspirants. Rachitha's dedication to empowering students is evident throughout this book.

Best Wishes

I wish all the readers the very best in their NEET journey and congratulate Rachitha on this remarkable achievement.

Prakash Y C

Principal and Senior Biology NEET Faculty

WHY IS THIS BOOK FOR YOU?

What if Biology didn't have to feel like a burden?

What if you could remember entire NCERT chapters — not by reading them ten times, but by *visualizing*, *sketching*, and *strategically recalling* them?

Welcome to a unique learning experience.

Welcome to **Make Learning An Innovation**.

The smart way to crack NEET through Biology and step into a White coat

This book is not just about memorizing facts for the NEET. It's about **reprogramming the way you learn** Biology. Inside, you'll discover tools and techniques that blend **neuroscience, coaching psychology, and creativity** to help you:

- Master NCERT Biology through **visual thinking**

- Retain complex topics with **memory palaces and mnemonics**

- Sketch your way to clearer understanding and longer retention

- Build **daily learning rituals** that make studying consistent and stress-free

- Apply everything in a **smart NEET revision system** designed for toppers

As a NEET Biology Mastery & Memory Coach, I've seen hundreds of students go from overwhelmed to confident — not by studying *harder*, but by studying *smarter*. This book captures everything I teach my students during my coaching sessions, visual workshops, and personal mentoring.

You'll find each chapter packed with strategies, examples, templates, and reflection activities — so that you're not just reading about these methods... you're actually using them.

Whether you're a first-time NEET aspirant, a repeater looking for a fresh approach, or a student who loves Biology but struggles with memory, this book is for you.

Because once you learn how your brain works, you'll never study the old way again.

So grab your colored pens, clear your desk, and get ready to turn Biology into a subject you'll not only understand but *remember for life*.

Let's make learning your superpower.

Coach Rachitha

NEET Biology Mastery and Memory coach

ABOUT THE AUTHOR

Coach Rachitha is a **NEET Biology Mastery and Memory Coach** who empowers students to master the NCERT using **brain-based learning strategies,** known for her creative methods, such as **mind maps, mnemonics, and memory palaces**, she helps aspirants learn faster, retain information longer, and revise more effectively. Through her work, hundreds of NEET students have transformed Biology from a subject of confusion into one of clarity by increasing their **speed of answering and accuracy** with Biology MCQ's and gaining considerable confidence to crack the NEET. With recognised awards for teaching excellence and passion for simplifying complex Biology concepts, **her mission is to shape unstoppable ethical doctors who drive healthier India.**

TABLE OF CONTENTS

Chapter 1: The Science of Memory & Visualization

1.1 Why This Chapter Matters?

Before diving into techniques, it's essential to understand *how* memory and visualization work? As a NEET Biology aspirant, you are dealing with massive information: processes, classifications, pathways, and diagrams.

Memorizing without understanding memory is like running a marathon without knowing how to breathe properly.

This chapter connects how your brain processes, stores, and recalls information, and how to use visualization to make Biology unforgettable.

****

1.2 A Quick Overview

Memory is the process of recalling information that you learned. Many parts of your brain work together to collect information and store it so you can find and access it when you need it.

Types of Memory

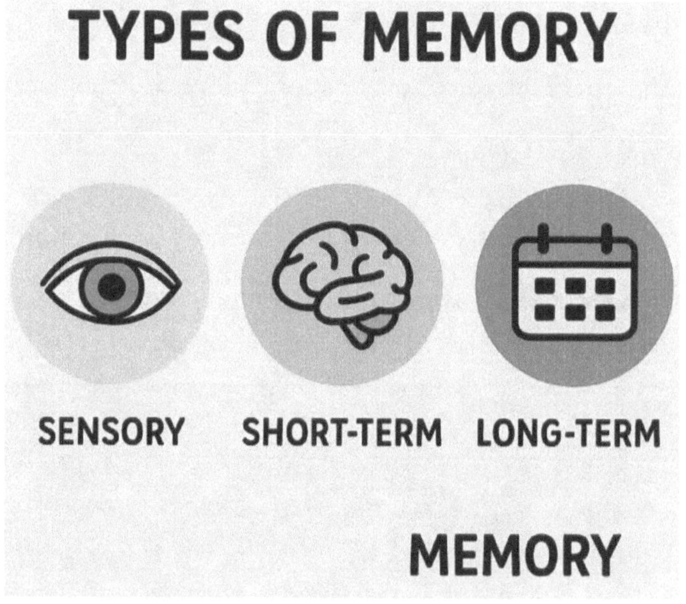

- **Sensory Memory:**

This is information collected from your senses (hearing, touch, smell, taste and vision). You only store it for couple of seconds. You don't consciously control this type of memory but it's highly detailed. E.g., you listen to a music—your brain captures it for a few milliseconds and it responds as expression.

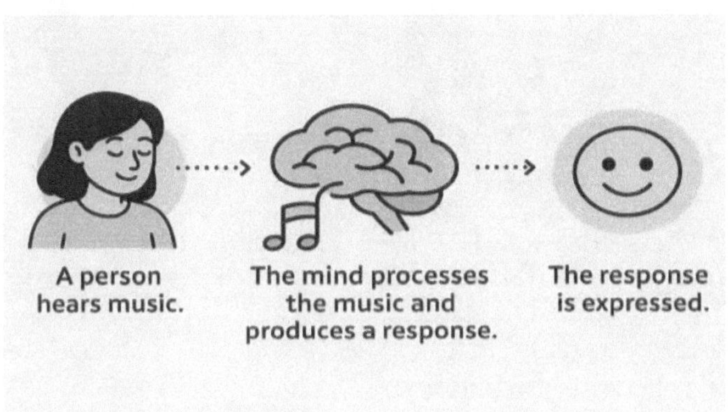

- **Short-Term Memory (STM):**

Holds limited information temporarily (15–30 seconds). Cramming works here—but not for NEET prep.

- **Long-Term Memory (LTM):**

The goal! Knowledge stored here can last days to years. To achieve this, we utilize repetition, emotion, and—most importantly—**visualization**.

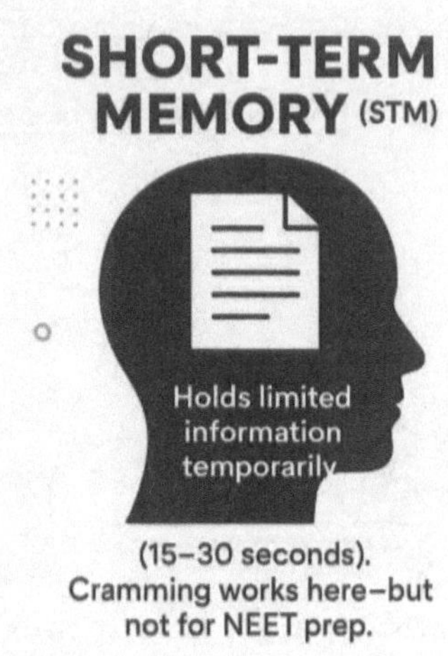

- **Working Memory:**

Actively used during thinking/problem solving. Strengthening this helps you think critically when taking multiple-choice questions (MCQs).

****

1.3 How the Brain Remembers: Key Concepts

ENCODING

- The process of converting information into a form that your brain can store.
- Visuals + emotions = stronger encoding

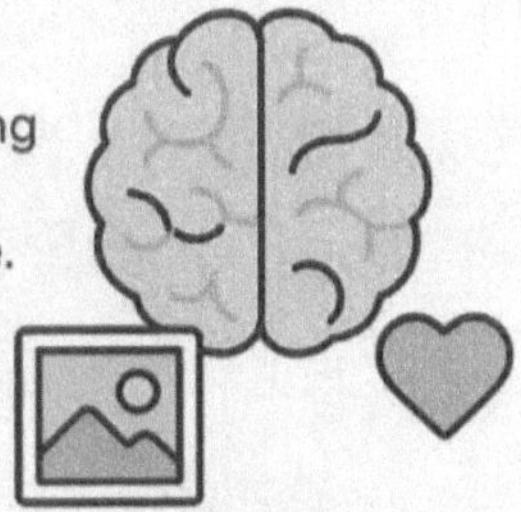

STORAGE

- Organized like a library.
- Mnemonics, mind maps, and patterns help organize biology content efficiently

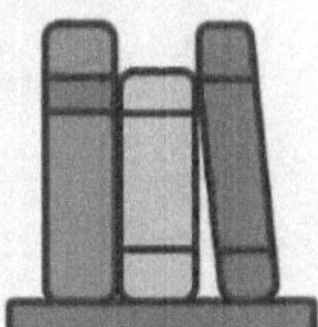

RETRIEVAL

- The act of recalling
- Active recall (quiz-based learning) boosts this

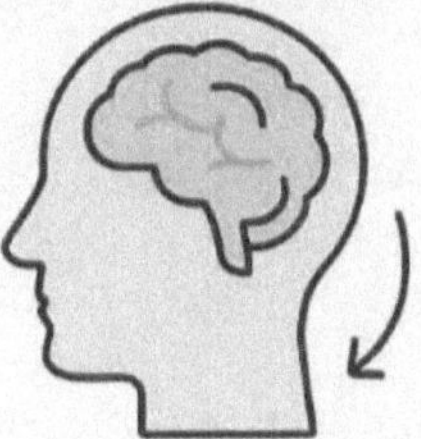

Fun Fact: Studies show that students retain **65% of visual information** three days later vs. only **10% of written/verbal info**.

****

1.4 The Power of Visualization in Biology

Visualization in Biology is a powerful tool that aids in understanding complex biological processes, communicating findings, and engaging in the scientific process. E.g. Think about DNA helices, human organs, plant anatomy, and ecological pyramids using mental image, color-coded notes, and diagram-based learning makes recall easy and retention longer.

Why Visualization Works:

- **Dual Coding Theory:**

  When you learn with both images and text, the brain creates two memory traces—doubling your recall potential.

- **Picture Superiority Effect:**

  Humans process images **60,000x faster** than text.

HOW VISUALS ARE STORED IN MEMORY

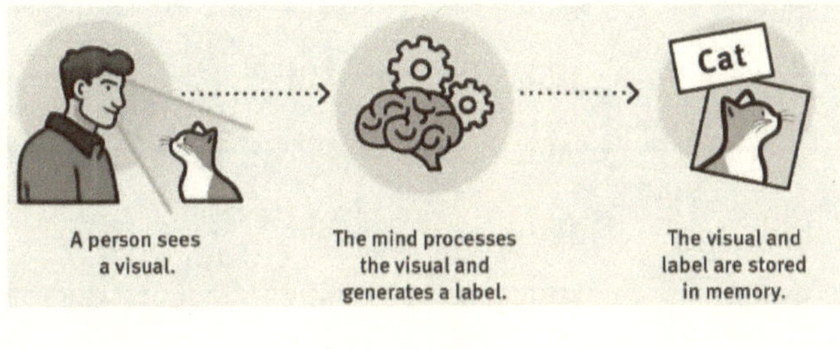

****

1.5 The Science Behind Mnemonics

Mnemonics turn dry info into catchy, colorful memories. You'll use acronyms, rhymes, absurd images, and storytelling to encode complex Biological facts (such as taxonomy, cranial nerves, or photosynthesis stages).

Example:

To remember the taxonomy order: **"King Philip Came Over For Good Soup"**

- Kingdom, Phylum, Class, Order, Family, Genus, Species

This takes a complex concept and embeds it in a funny, visual story in your brain.

****

1.6 Visual Thinking vs. Rote Learning

Rote Learning	Visual Learning
Repetitive & boring	Creative & engaging
High forgetting curve	Long-lasting memory
Passive	Active
Ineffective in stress	Easy recall under pressure

1.7 Your Brain is Wired for Patterns

Biology is full of patterns—homologous structures, feedback loops, and genetic codes.

When you visualize these as shapes, flows, or icons, your brain *recognizes* them more easily than trying to *remember* them.

****

1.8 Quick Brain Boosts to Improve Memory

- **Chunking:** Break large amounts of content into smaller groups (e.g., types of immunity).

- **Storytelling:** Turn Biology facts into mini-stories.

- **Mind Mapping:** Create a central image and expand with branches—ideal for systems like Circulatory, Nervous, etc.

- **Teaching Others:** Explaining concepts helps solidify your understanding and strengthens your memory.

****

1.9 Takeaway

In this book, you'll learn to **study with your brain, not against it.** By understanding how memory and visualization work, you're now ready to apply them to your NEET Biology preparation—strategically and effectively.

****

Reflection Activity

Before moving to Chapter 2, try this:

- Choose a Biology topic (e.g., Photosynthesis).

- Please close your eyes and visualize it as a *movie scene* or *storyboard*.

- Draw a rough sketch of that visualization.

- Now, try explaining the topic aloud based on your sketch.

That's the beginning of *Bio-Visualization Mastery*.

Chapter 2: Foundations of Smart Learning

2.1 Introduction: Study Smarter, Not Harder

The biggest trap NEET aspirants fall into is **information overload**. Many students think the more hours they study, the better. But it's not about how long you study—it's about *how* you study. Smart learning is all about optimizing memory, focus, and retention through techniques that align with how your brain works.

This chapter introduces the core tools — **Active Recall, Spaced Repetition**, and **Learning Styles** — and explains how to create a daily structure that supports long-term retention.

****

2.2 Know Thyself: Discover Your Learning Style

Everyone learns differently. Some students absorb information more effectively through visuals, while others learn better through auditory or kinesthetic experiences. Identifying your **dominant learning style** helps you select the most effective memory technique for your needs.

4 Primary Learning Styles:

- **Visual (Spatial):** Learns best through images, diagrams, colours, and videos. (Ideal for sketching biology pathways!)

- **Auditory:** Learns through sound, music, and discussions. (Try voice notes and teaching aloud.)

- **Reading/Writing:** Prefers text, notes, and lists. (Summarizing from the NCERT works best.)

- **Kinesthetic:** Learns through movement, touch, and hands-on activities. (Best for model-making, practical demos.)

Activity:

Take 5 minutes to reflect or complete an online quiz to determine your dominant learning style. Write it down—you'll use it in later chapters.

****

2.3 Active Recall: The #1 Learning Hack

Most students read and re-read the NCERT, but forget it in 3 days. Why? Because passive reading doesn't activate memory.

Active recall means testing yourself *before* you feel ready. It forces your brain to retrieve info, which strengthens memory pathways.

How to Use It in Biology:

- After studying Plant Physiology, close your book and write down everything you remember.

- Use **flashcards**, quizzes, or teach a friend.

- Focus on pulling information *out* of your brain, not just putting it in.

Pro Tip: Use the **"blurting method"** — write all you remember on paper after a topic, then compare with your notes.

****

2.4 Spaced Repetition: Beat the Forgetting Curve

Even if you understand something today, you'll forget most of it in a week if you don't revise.

Spaced Repetition is a technique where you review information at increasing intervals:

1 Day > 3 Days > 7 Days > 14 Days > 30 Days

Tools to Automate It:

- **Anki** – a flashcard app that uses spaced repetition.

- **Notion** or **Google Sheets** – create a simple revision tracker.

- **Calendar Method** – schedule weekly topic reviews.

****

2.5 Smart Note-Making for Biology

Notebooks shouldn't be a copy of your NCERT. They should be **memory tools.**

Effective Notes Should:

- Include **diagrams** and **flowcharts** wherever possible.

- Use **colours** to code systems (e.g., green for plant biology, red for circulatory).

- Use **keywords, symbols**, and **arrows** instead of long paragraphs.

Pro Tip: Dedicate one page per topic with condensed points, visual cues, and mnemonics.

****

2.6 The Role of the Environment in Learning

Your brain associate's memory with **location, sound, and state of mind**. Studying in chaos makes memory chaotic.

Tips for a Brain-Friendly Study Environment:

- Keep your desk clutter-free.

- Use calming background music (if auditory).

- Turn off phone notifications.

- Study in blocks of **25-30 minutes (Pomodoro technique)** with 5-minute breaks.

****

2.7 The Power of Routine

Memory thrives on consistency. Instead of cramming for 6 hours once, study for one focused hour every day.

Sample Daily Study Routine for Biology:

Time	Activity
7:00–7:30 AM	Review notes from yesterday (Spaced Repetition)
4:00–5:00 PM	Study a new topic with visual techniques.
9:00–9:30 PM	Active recall session / blurting method

Overtime, this becomes *automatic*, which reduces stress and increases retention.

****

2.8 Combine Techniques: Your Learning Toolkit

Let's connect everything so far:

Goal	Tool
Understand fast	Mind maps, diagrams
Remember long-term	Spaced repetition

Recall during exams	Active recall
Learn with ease	Visuals + mnemonics
Stay consistent	Daily routine, Pomodoro, notes

2.9 Quick Wins: What You Can Start Today

- Pick one topic (e.g., Photosynthesis)

- Create a **1-page mind map**

- Write five active recall questions

- Schedule 3 revisions using the spaced method

- Stick the mind map on your wall

You've already started learning smarter!

****

2.10 Final Thoughts

You don't need a photographic memory to crack NEET Biology. You need a **strategic system** that works with your brain, not against it. Smart learning combines science with self-awareness. Now that you've built your foundation, it's time to explore specific memory tools—starting with mnemonics, mind maps, and visual learning in the next chapters.

Chapter 3: Mnemonics Made Easy for Biology

3.1 What Are Mnemonics and Why Do They Work?

Mnemonics are memory aids that help you **condense large amounts of information** into a concise, memorable format. Your brain loves **patterns, rhymes, and visual triggers**—mnemonics tap into all three.

Whether it's remembering the order of classification or cranial nerves, mnemonics transform "boring lists" into "brain candy."

Scientific Basis:

Mnemonics use **association and emotional connection**, which trigger stronger encoding in your brain. When you create a humorous or unusual association, the brain pays attention and stores it more deeply.

****

3.2 Types of Mnemonics You'll Learn

Here are five powerful types of mnemonics tailored for NEET Biology:

1. **Acronyms** – Using initials to form a word or phrase.

2. **Acrostics** – First letters form a sentence.

3. **Rhymes & Songs** – Rhythm boosts memory.

4. **Chunking** – Breaking info into smaller groups.

5. **Image Mnemonics** – Associating a fact with a vivid mental picture.

****

3.3 Classic Examples for NEET Biology

Let's break down some examples by topic.

1. Taxonomy Order (Classification Hierarchy)

Kingdom, Phylum, Class, Order, Family, Genus, Species

Mnemonic: *King Philip Came Over For Good Soup*

2. Cranial Nerves (Names)

Mnemonic: *Oh Oh Oh To Touch And Feel Very Green Vegetables And Herbs*

(Corresponds to: Olfactory, Optic, Oculomotor, Trochlear...)

3. Essential Amino Acids

Mnemonic: *HILL Makes Tall Vampires Fear Less*

(Histidine, Isoleucine, Leucine, Lysine, Methionine, Threonine, Valine, Phenylalanine, etc.)

4. Plant Hormones

Mnemonic: *ABC-EG*

(Auxin, Brassinosteroids, Cytokinin, Ethylene, Gibberellins)

5. Mitosis Stages

Mnemonic: *I Passed My Anatomy Test Calmly*

(Interphase, Prophase, Metaphase, Anaphase, Telophase, Cytokinesis)

****

3.4 How to Create Your Own Mnemonics (Step-by-Step)

Creating your mnemonics is even more powerful than using existing ones—it engages your brain in a creative process, which in turn boosts your memory.

Step-by-Step Guide:

1. **Choose the list or concept you want to memorize.**

2. **Pick the first letter of each word.**

3. **Rearrange into a funny phrase, sentence, or image.**

4. **Add emotion, humor, or exaggeration.**

5. **Say it out loud, draw it, or teach it.**

Example: To remember the steps of aerobic respiration (Glycolysis → Link Reaction → Krebs Cycle → ETC), create:

"Great Lions Kill Every Tiger Calmly."

****

3.5 Visualization + Mnemonics = Superpower

Don't stop at words—**visualize the mnemonic.**

Try This:

For mitosis:

"I Passed My Anatomy Test Calmly"

Now, picture a **student passing through different doors** in a biology lab:

- **Interphase** – relaxing in a library

- **Prophase** – everything becomes tangled

- **Metaphase** – books line up

- **Anaphase** – books get pulled apart

- **Telophase** – things settle down

- **Cytokinesis** – leaving the lab as two students

This turns abstract steps into a **mental story**.

****

3.6 Student-Created Mnemonics Wall

Now try to create mnemonics and share them with your peers. This builds an emotional connection and collaborative memory.

Create a "Mnemonic Wall":

- Have a sticky note corner (digital or physical)

- Add a new mnemonic every day

* Review weekly with friends

****

3.7 Common Pitfalls to Avoid

* **Too Complex:** Keep it short and simple.

* **No Visual Link:** Always create a visual or evoke an emotion.

* **Using Someone Else's Mnemonic Without Meaning:** If you didn't create it, personalize it somehow.

* **Forgetting to Revise:** Mnemonics Still Need Spaced Repetition!

****

3.8 Apply It Now: Your Mnemonic Challenge

Pick a difficult list from your current syllabus (e.g., enzymes in digestion, blood vessels of the heart, plant tissues). Now:

* Make a visual mnemonic

* Draw it

* Say it aloud

- Stick it near your study space

Bonus: Teach it to a friend.

****

3.9 Final Thoughts

Mnemonics are not shortcuts—they're **smart-cuts.**

They don't replace understanding; they **enhance recall**.

When combined with visualization and active recall, they create an unbeatable Biology memory strategy.

****

Quick Summary Box

Topic	Mnemonic Style	Example
Taxonomy	Acrostic	*King Philip Came Over For Good Soup*
Mitosis	Phrase + Story	*I Passed My Anatomy Test Calmly*
Hormones	Acronym	*ABC-EG*
Nerves	Phrase	*Oh Oh Oh To Touch...*
Your turn	Create one!	(Student Activity)

Chapter 4: The Art of Mind Mapping Biology Concepts

4.1 What Is a Mind Map?

A **mind map** is a visual representation of information structured around a central concept. Instead of reading linearly (like a textbook), it allows your brain to *see* how concepts are **connected**, making complex Biology topics easier to remember and revise.

Mind mapping is one of the most effective tools for visual learners and is particularly well-suited for NCERT-based Biology.

****

4.2 Why Mind Mapping Works for Biology

Biology is full of **hierarchies, systems, processes, and relationships**. Mind maps convert these into a **visual format** that your brain can quickly absorb and recall.

Benefits:

- Organizes scattered topics into one visual frame

- Boosts retention by activating both logic and creativity

- Helps in quick revision before exams

- Makes long chapters less overwhelming

****

4.3 Basic Elements of a Mind Map

1. **Central Idea:**

2. Place the main topic in the centre (e.g., *Respiratory System*).

3. **Branches:**

4. Create thick branches for subtopics (e.g., Human Respiratory Tract, Mechanism of Breathing, Regulation).

5. **Keywords & Phrases:**

6. Use only **essential words**, not long sentences.

7. **Colours & Symbols:**

8. Different colours for branches help in memory. Use arrows, icons, and doodles to enhance your message.

9. **Images & Diagrams:**

10. Sketch small visuals where possible (e.g., alveoli, lungs, oxygen exchange).

****

4.4 Step-by-Step: How to Create a Biology Mind Map

Let's go through an example for **Photosynthesis**.

Step 1: Write "Photosynthesis" in the centre and draw a sun icon.

Step 2: Add main branches:

- Light Reaction

- Dark Reaction

- Chloroplast Structure

- Factors Affecting Photosynthesis

- Pigments

Step 3: On each branch, add keywords like:

- Light Reaction → PSII, Electron Transport, ATP, NADPH

- Pigments → Chlorophyll a, b, carotenoids

Step 4: Add small diagrams (e.g., Z-scheme for light reaction).

Step 5: Use colour codes:

- Blue for processes

- Green for structures

- Red for conditions

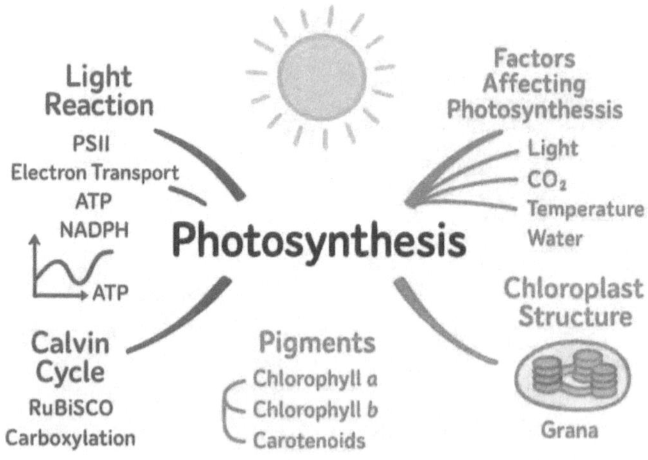

Result: You've now turned eight textbook pages into a **1-page memory masterpiece.**

****

4.5 Where to Use Mind Maps in NEET Biology

Mind maps work well in:

- **Human Physiology:** Digestive, Respiratory, Nervous Systems

- **Plant Physiology:** Photosynthesis, Transport, Growth

- **Cell Biology:** Organelles, Cell Cycle, Biomolecules

- **Genetics & Evolution:** Mendelian laws, DNA replication

- **Ecology:** Pyramids, Cycles, Biodiversity

****

4.6 Digital vs. Handwritten Mind Maps

Format	Pros	Tools
Handwritten	Boosts creativity, better memory	Pen & paper, colour pens
Digital	Clean, editable, shareable	XMind, Canva, MindMeister

Pro Tip: Start with hand-drawn maps, then digitize for final revision.

****

4.7 Mind Mapping for Revision

Here's a **Weekly Revision Hack**:

- Create a 1-page mind map for every chapter you finish.

- On Sunday, revise three mind maps instead of reading 30 pages.

- Before exams, revise *only mind maps + mnemonics.*

****

4.8 Common Mistakes to Avoid

- **Overloading with text** – Stick to keywords only

- **Messy layout** – Organize branches logically

- **No visual elements** – Add icons or diagrams for better retention

- **Using it just once** – Revisit and revise regularly

****

4.9 Activity: Make Your First Mind Map

Pick a topic: (e.g., *Human Circulatory System*)

Steps:

- Draw a central circle and label it

- Create 5–7 main branches

- Add 2–3 keywords or diagrams per branch

- Use at least three colours

- Time yourself (20–30 min max)

Stick it on your wall, use it for active recall tomorrow.

****

4.10 Final Thoughts

Mind maps are your secret weapon for visualizing, **revising, and retaining information**. Every NEET Biology topper uses *some form of visual organization*—so why not master it early?

Remember:

"If you can map it, you can remember it."

****

"If you can map it, you can remember it."

Bonus: Chapter Recap — Quick Mind Map Formula

Step	Action
1	Choose a central concept
2	Branch subtopics
3	Add keywords, diagrams.
4	Use colors/symbols
5	Review regularly

Chapter 5: Visualizing Biology – Sketching for Memory

5.1 Why Sketching Matters in Biology?

Have you noticed how NEET Biology is packed with diagrams? That's not by accident. Biology is inherently **visual, encompassing** organs, cells, feedback loops, structures, and processes. But here's the twist: instead of just *seeing* diagrams, students should start *creating* them.

Sketching activates active learning—you process information more deeply when you draw it yourself. You don't need to be an artist. You need to represent what you understand using **simple shapes and labels**.

****

5.2 How Drawing Boosts Memory

- **Active Engagement:** Forces your brain to make sense of what you're learning.

- **Dual Coding:** You remember better when you use words and images together.

- **Motor Memory:** Drawing physically wires the information into your brain.

- **Emotional Connection:** A diagram you draw yourself becomes yours, not just something from a book.

****

5.3 3 Levels of Biology Sketching

Level 1: Copying from the Textbook

- First, observe and copy the NCERT diagrams

- Use this stage to get familiar with proportions and parts

Level 2: Redrawing from Memory

- After studying a topic, try drawing it without looking

- Fill in what you remember first, then add the missing parts

- Great for **active recall**

Level 3: Creative Sketching for Concepts

- Turn concepts into **simple metaphors**

- E.g., Mitochondria as a power station synthesizing ATP

- This is *visual storytelling*, not technical art

MITOCHONDRIA AS POWER STATION

****

5.4 How to Start Drawing Biology Concepts (Even if You Can't Draw)

Here's the good news—you don't need to draw *realistically*. You need to draw *memorably*.

Keep It Simple:

- Use **basic shapes** (circles, lines, arrows, boxes)

- Add labels clearly

- Use **symbols** (heart for circulation, gear for feedback mechanism)

Example:

- For the **Human Heart**, draw a simple 4-box structure with arrows for blood flow.

- Add blue arrows for deoxygenated areas and red arrows for oxygenated areas.

- Label atria, ventricles, and valves with short forms.

SIMPLE SKETCH OF HUMAN HEART

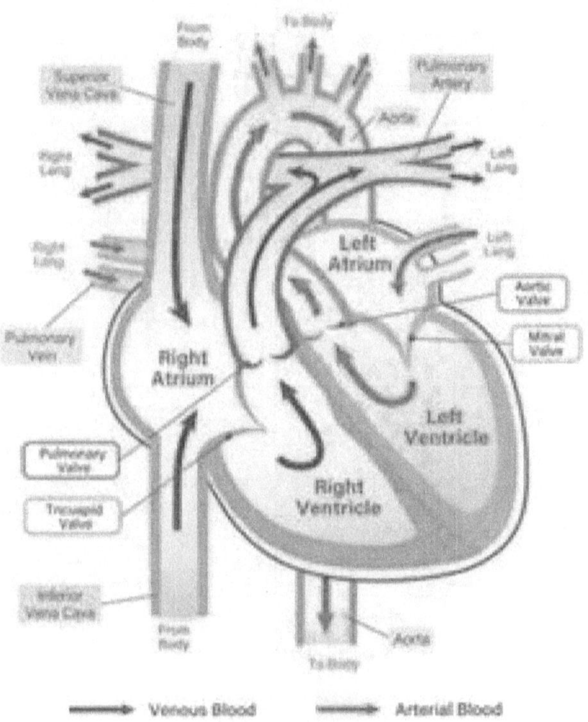

****

5.5 Visual Tools That Work Well in Biology

Tool	Use Case	Example
Flowcharts	Processes, pathways	Glycolysis, Immunity
Diagrams	Structures	Heart, Nephron, Chloroplast
Timelines	Developmental stages	Embryogenesis
Cycles	Repetitive processes	Menstrual Cycle, Calvin Cycle
Tables	Comparisons	Monocot vs Dicot, DNA vs RNA

5.6 Add Emotion and Humour for Stickiness

Funny or exaggerated visuals stick longer.

Examples:

- Draw a chloroplast as a *green chef* cooking glucose using sunlight.

CHLOROPLAST AS GREEN CHEF

- Sketch enzymes as *keys* opening *locks* on substrates.

- Imagine the brain as a Wi-Fi router, managing signals throughout the nervous system.

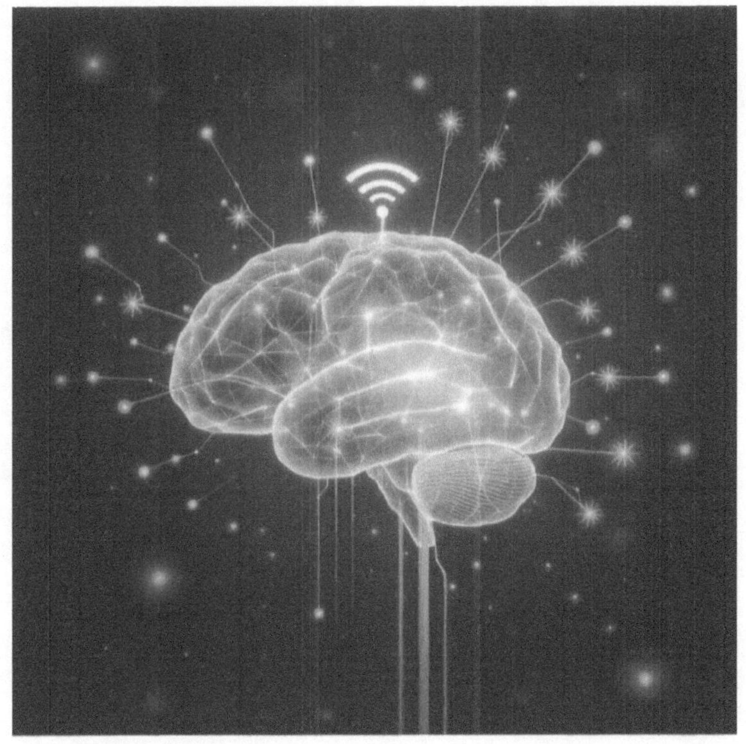

This brings boring topics to life and makes revision ten times more enjoyable.

****

5.7 Create a Visual Notes Folder

Start a "Visual Biology Vault":

- Dedicate a notebook or digital folder to just diagrams

- One page = One topic = One visual

- Revise from this visual bank regularly

Bonus Tip: After every major chapter, draw a *1-page summary diagram* of the whole unit.

****

5.8 Combine Sketching with Mnemonics and Mind Maps

Use **mnemonics** for labels and **mind map branching** to structure the sketch.

Example: For the nervous system:

- Central node = Brain

- Branch out: Cerebrum, Cerebellum, Spinal Cord

- Add small sketches + mnemonics for the function

Now you're mixing three powerful tools—sketching, mapping, and memory cues.

****

5.9 Activity: Sketch Your Concept

Choose a topic (e.g., Nephron, Carbon Cycle, Synapse).

1. Read it once.

2. Close the book.

3. Draw from memory.

4. Use colours, labels, and arrows to enhance clarity and readability.

5. Stick it in your visual vault.

Challenge yourself: Can you explain it to someone using *just your sketch*?

****

5.10 Final Thoughts

Sketching makes learning Biology **interactive, engaging, and unforgettable**.

You don't need to be an artist—you need a pen, a page, and a willingness to experiment.

Your brain will thank you for every shape, arrow, and stick figure you draw.

"If you can draw it, you can remember it."

****

Quick Recap Box: Sketching in NEET Biology

Strategy	Purpose
Redraw from memory	Strengthens recall
Use shapes/symbols	Simplifies complex ideas
Create metaphors	Builds emotional connection
Maintain a sketch vault.	Fast revision

Chapter 6: Creating Memory Palaces for Biology Topics

6.1 What Is a Memory Palace?

A **Memory Palace** is a powerful visualization technique used by memory champions, ancient scholars, and now NEET aspirants!

It's a mental "building" (like your home, school, or even a fantasy castle) where you **store facts in specific locations**. Each room or object holds a different piece of information. When you mentally "walk" through it, you recall everything in sequence.

It works because your brain remembers *places and images* far better than abstract facts.

****

6.2 Why It Works (And Why It's Perfect for Biology)

- **Leverages spatial memory** – humans evolved to remember locations

- **Creates strong mental connections** using images, colours, and emotion

- **Ideal for sequences and categories** – think taxonomy, classification, processes, etc.

- **Fun and stress-free** – revising feels like a form of storytelling.

****

6.3 How to Build a Memory Palace (Step-by-Step)

Step 1: Choose a familiar location

Pick a place you know well: your house, your school, your street, or even your favourite café. This becomes the "palace" for that chapter.

Step 2: Assign a topic to each room or area

E.g., if you're storing the **Digestive System**, each room holds a part:

- Kitchen = Mouth & Salivary Glands

- Dining Room = Esophagus

- Hall = Stomach

- Bedroom = Small Intestine

- Balcony = Large Intestine

Step 3: Place visual cues in each room

Imagine exaggerated, funny, or emotional images:

- On your kitchen counter: a giant tongue licking sugar = salivary amylase

- In the hall: a **blender** filled with acid = HCl, and pepsin in the stomach

- In the bedroom: a **sponge bed** absorbing food = villi in the small intestine

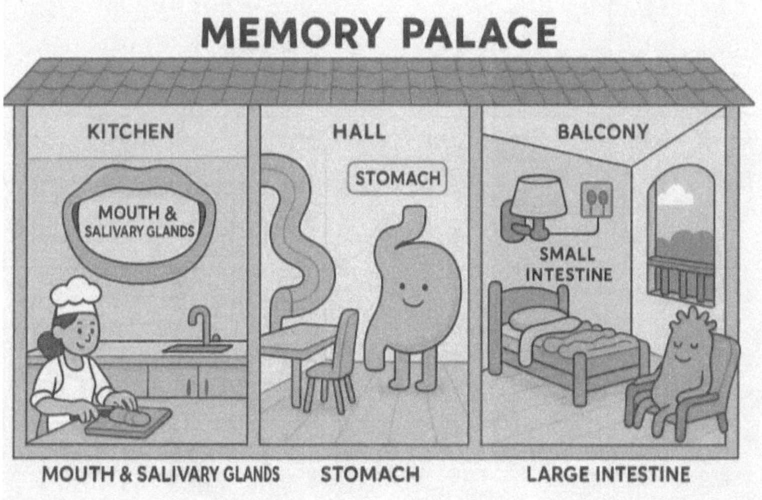

Step 4: Walk through your palace to recall

Close your eyes, mentally walk through, and "see" each fact in its place.

****

6.4 Real-Life Example: Memory Palace for Photosynthesis

Let's store the **Photosynthesis** chapter in your **school building**:

Area	Topic	Visual Clue
School gate	Light energy enters	Giant sun above the gate
Chemistry lab	Light Reaction	Bursting test tubes = ATP & NADPH
Biology lab	Calvin Cycle	A spinning sugar machine
Library	Factors affecting photosynthesis	Book of "CO2, Light & Temperature"
Staff room	Pigments	Teachers painted green!

During revision, take a mental tour of your school—you'll remember the entire process without touching the textbook.

****

6.5 Tips to Make Your Memory Palace Stick

- Use **weird, emotional, or exaggerated images** (the crazier, the better!)

- Always use places you know well to reduce confusion

- Create **separate palaces** for different chapters or units

- **Draw a map** of your palace to aid practice

- Use **voice recordings** to walk yourself through your palace aloud

****

6.6 Best Topics for Biology Memory Palaces

Ideal for	Examples
Sequences & Steps	Photosynthesis, Digestion, Immunity, Menstrual Cycle
Classifications	Taxonomy, Plant Families, Animal Phyla
Lists & Names	Enzymes, Hormones, Cranial Nerves, Disorders
Complex Interactions	Feedback loops, Respiration steps, Genetics laws

6.7 Activity: Create Your First Biology Palace

Topic: Human Circulatory System

Palace: Your house

- Door: Heart (beating doorbell)

- Hall: Arteries (red carpet rushing forward)

- Sofa: Veins (blue cushions bringing back stuff)

- Dining table: Capillaries (mesh of fine forks and spoons)

- Washroom: Pulmonary circulation (steam representing oxygen exchange)

Now, walk through it. Can you explain circulation without your book? That's the power of a Memory Palace!

****

6.8 Combine Palaces with Other Tools

- Use **mind maps** to sketch the layout of your palace.

- Add **mnemonics** into objects (e.g., the "King Philip..." mnemonic carved into a wall for taxonomy)

- Use **sketching** to draw parts of your palace or the visual clues

This creates a **multi-sensory, multi-layered memory** that's almost impossible to forget.

6.9 Common Mistakes to Avoid

- **Making it too realistic:** Add drama and exaggeration for memory

- **Overloading one room:** Keep one topic per space

- **Skipping visualization:** You must *see* it clearly in your mind

- **Not revisiting the palace regularly:** Practice = permanence

****

6.10 Final Thoughts

The Memory Palace technique turns your **mind into a revision tool**. With practice, you can walk through chapters like you're giving a campus tour of your memory. Creative. Fun. Effective.

"Your brain is a mansion. Why leave your notes outside?"

Quick Recap Box: Build a Biology Memory Palace

Step	Action
1	Choose a familiar location
2	Assign a topic per room.
3	Place funny visual clues.
4	Take a mental walkthrough.
5	Practice weekly for mastery.

Chapter 7: Daily Rituals to Boost Retention

7.1 The Myth of "Big Study Days"

Many students believe they need *long, exhausting study sessions* to succeed. However, science suggests otherwise: **small, focused, and consistent routines** are far more effective for memory retention, especially in subjects like Biology that rely heavily on memory.

Just like fitness, your brain improves with *daily reps*, not occasional marathons.

****

7.2 What Are Learning Rituals?

Rituals are **tiny, repeatable actions** that cue your brain to focus, remember, and recall. When linked with smart strategies like **active recall, visualization, spaced repetition, and sketching**, they become a powerful learning system.

These rituals help:

- Eliminate procrastination

- Reduce stress before exams

- Reinforce long-term memory

- Build study momentum

****

7.3 The 3 Golden Learning Times in a Day

Your brain has *natural windows* when it is more alert and ready to absorb information. Plan your study rituals around these for maximum memory retention.

7.4 Your NEET Biology Daily Ritual Plan

Let's build a **Biology Boosting Routine** around memory techniques you've already learned:

Time	Ritual Type	Why It Works
Morning (4–6 AM)	Deep Learning	Great for focused study
Evening (6–7 PM)	Review & Recall	Fresh brain, high retention
Night (9–9:30 PM)	Revision & Reflection	Solidifies memory before sleep

Morning (Focused Study – 1 hour)

- **New Topic + Visual Tools:** Study one new topic using a mind map or sketch.

- **Use Mnemonics:** Create a fun mnemonic on the spot.

- **Write 5 Recall Questions** for this topic to test later.

Evening (Recall- 30 minutes)

- **Spaced Repetition:** Revise 2–3 topics from the past week using flashcards or the blurting method.

- **Mind Map Review:** Look at one visual map or diagram on your wall.

- **Voice Note Recap:** Record or speak aloud what you remember.

Night (Memory Lockdown – 30 mins)

- **Recall Ritual:** Try to draw on memory or teach it to someone.

- **Quick Test:** Use the questions you asked earlier to quiz yourself. (Solve at least 10 MCQs)

- **Write Journal Entry:** One line: *"Today I remembered..."*

****

7.5 Weekend Ritual: The Bio-Revision Hour

Every weekend, set aside 1 hour for "memory gym":

- Review all the mind maps made that week

- Redo two key diagrams without looking

- Revisit old mnemonics and add new ones

- Solve 10 MCQs from the topics revised

- Reflect: What's one area I need to reinforce next week?

****

7.6 Rituals for Stress-Free Exam Prep

Stress kills memory. Rituals reduce anxiety by giving your brain predictability.

Before any mock test or exam:

- Do a 5-minute **mental visualization** of your strongest topics

- Carry a **pocket-sized sketch/cheat sheet** (diagrams + mnemonics only)

- Avoid cramming — instead, **recite five core concepts aloud**

****

7.7 Stack Rituals into Your Existing Life

You don't need extra time—you need smart habits.

Try "Habit Stacking":

- After brushing → Recall yesterday's topic

- During breakfast, → Listen to a short voice note summary

- While walking, → Mentally quiz yourself

- Before sleep → Draw or visualize one diagram in your head

These micro-moments can revolutionize your memory.

****

7.8 Make It Fun: Ritual Gamification

Make your rituals enjoyable so they stick!

- **Memory Jar:** Drop a sticky note in a jar for every concept you recall perfectly

- **Sketch & Share:** Post your best diagram or mnemonic weekly

- **Biology Bingo:** Make a card of tasks (e.g., "Draw the heart", "Create a plant hormone mnemonic") and check them off

- **Track Progress:** Use a sticker chart or app to reward consistency

****

7.9 Ritual Tracker Template

Time	Task	Done? (✔)
Morning	Learn a new concept visually.	
Morning	Spaced revision	
Evening	Review the mind map	
Night	Sketch from memory	
Night	Reflect in the journal.	

Print this and stick it in your study space—it becomes your accountability buddy.

****

7.10 Final Thoughts

Success in NEET Biology isn't about doing more—it's about doing the **right things daily**. These rituals turn every day into a small victory. Slowly, they stack into total mastery.

"Excellence is not an act, but a habit."

The chapters ahead will show you how to apply these rituals to full NCERT chapters, exam prep strategies, and real-life case studies from NEET toppers.

Chapter 8: Integrating Techniques into NEET Prep

8.1 From Tools to Strategy

You've learned the tools:

- Mind maps

- Mnemonics

- Sketching

- Memory palaces

- Spaced repetition

- Active recall

- Daily rituals

Now let's **embed these tools into your NEET preparation—** not as "extras" but as **your default way of learning**.

This chapter serves as your **implementation guide** for utilizing these techniques in conjunction with **NCERT Biology**, past-year questions, and mock tests.

****

8.2 NCERT: Your Core Material

NCERT is the **Bible for NEET Biology**. Nearly 95% of questions are based on it. Your job is not just to *read* it—it's to **internalize** it.

Here's how to make NCERT your memory playground:

Step-by-Step NEET Biology Study Strategy:

1. **Read the NCERT topic once passively**

2. **Highlight keywords** (use different colours for definitions, diagrams, and examples)

3. **Immediately draw a visual summary** – sketch or mind map

4. **Create mnemonics** for lists, sequences, or exceptions

5. **Test yourself using active recall** – write or say aloud what you remember

6. **Schedule revision** using spaced repetition (1 day > 3 days > 7 days > 14 days > monthly)

****

8.3 Visualizing a Full NCERT Chapter: Example – "Human Reproduction"

Topic	Technique	Example
Male reproductive system	Sketch + labelling	Draw and label from memory
Hormonal regulation	Memory Palace	Imagine a hospital controlling hormones
Menstrual cycle	Flowchart + mnemonics	"OELM" (Ovulation, Estrogen, Luteal, Menstruation)
Fertilization	Story method	A sperm's "journey" as an adventure cartoon
Embryo development	Timeline chart	Day-by-day breakdown

This way, a 15-page chapter becomes four pages of visuals, three mnemonics, one story, and a permanent memory.

****

8.4 Apply Tools to MCQ Practice

Memorization is only half the game. You must also train your brain to **retrieve and apply knowledge under exam conditions.**

Here's How:

- After every new topic, solve **10 MCQs** from that chapter

- Mark the incorrect ones and **map them to your visual notes**

- Create a **"Mistake Tracker"** and add visual or mnemonic fixes

Example:

You forget the role of LH in the menstrual cycle. Add a cartoon of "LH as the Luteinizing Hero" to your mind map.

****

8.5 Creating a 30-60-90 Day NEET Biology Plan

Phase 1: First 30 Days – Build the Foundation

- Cover 1–2 chapters per day

- Create visual notes, mnemonics, and mind maps

- Use daily recall rituals and active testing

Phase 2: Next 30 Days – Strengthen Memory

- Revise all chapters once using **sketches + flashcards**

- Practice 20–30 MCQs per day

- Complete your **Memory Palace** maps and revisit them

Phase 3: Last 30 Days – Exam-Ready Revision

- Daily mixed-topic MCQ tests

- Revise ONLY from visuals and summaries

- Avoid new content, focus on **speed + accuracy**

****

8.6 Case Study: Topper's Strategy Using These Techniques

Name: Riya Sharma

NEET Score: 355/360 in Biology

Tools Used:

- Draw 1 diagram per topic every day

- Made 60+ mnemonics for plant physiology

- Reviewed all visuals before sleep

- Built a memory palace for animal classification

- Revised full syllabus 4 times with mind maps only

Result? **Fast recall + zero last-minute panic.**

****

8.7 Smart Use of Technology

Combine your manual techniques with digital tools:

Tool	Use
Anki	Spaced flashcards
Notion	Visual revision dashboard

| Canva | Design pretty mind maps or infographic notes. |
| Google Calendar | Schedule your 90-day prep plan. |

Utilize these tools to **automate revisions** and maintain visually rich content.

****

8.8 Templates You Can Use

- **Weekly Memory Planner** – Plan which topics to sketch, recall, and test

- **Mistake Fixer Sheet** – Track wrong MCQs and how you fixed them

- **Mind Map Folder** – Organize by NCERT chapter

- **Mnemonic Wall** – Add one new mnemonic per day

These become your **Biology toolkit,** you'll rely on throughout your prep.

****

8.9 From Confusion to Clarity: Mindset Shift

Before:

- "There's too much to memorize."

- "I keep forgetting diagrams."

- "Revision is boring."

After:

- "I have a visual for every chapter."

- "My sketches help me recall instantly."

- "I enjoy revising—it feels like reviewing my art gallery."

Your new identity: **I am a Visual Biology Learner.**

****

8.10 Final Thoughts

Your NEET Biology prep is no longer about stress, fear, or endless revision. It's about **strategy, creativity, and smart recall.** Every tool you've learned now fits into a system.

This chapter isn't just about studying. It's about taking full **ownership** of your prep—and turning your mind into a Biology machine.

"Don't just study Biology. *Live it visually. Learn it creatively. Recall it confidently.*"

Chapter 9: Mistakes Students Make And How to Avoid Them

9.1 Why This Chapter Matters

Many NEET aspirants *work hard* but still feel stuck or overwhelmed. Often, it's not about a lack of effort, but **inefficient methods**. This chapter is a reality check. It exposes the most common study traps and provides you with **visual, strategic, and mindset-based solutions** to address them quickly.

****

9.2 Mistake #1: Blind Rote Learning

The Problem:

Students try to memorize everything *line by line* from the NCERT without understanding or connecting ideas.

Why It Fails:

- No deep learning

- Poor long-term retention

- Panic during tricky MCQs

Fix It:

- Use **mind maps** to understand how topics connect

- Apply **mnemonics** to lists and facts

- **Sketch processes** to lock them visually

Example: Instead of rote memorizing the steps of Glycolysis, draw it as a *factory* with glucose entering and ATP being packed and shipped out.

****

9.3 Mistake #2: Ignoring Diagrams

The Problem:

Students often skip drawing or fail to label the NCERT diagrams properly.

Why It Fails:

- NEET loves **label-based diagram MCQs**

- Misses out on visual memory pathways

Fix It:

- Practice **diagram recall weekly**

- Add **coloured visual notes** beside each diagram

- **Sketch from memory** after studying

Pro Tip: Make a "Top 30 Diagrams" wall with stick sketches of key NCERT visuals.

****

9.4 Mistake #3: Cramming Before Exams

The Problem:

Waiting until the last few weeks to revise the whole syllabus in panic mode.

Why It Fails:

- High stress, low retention

- Incomplete revision

- Mind blanks during the exam

Fix It:

- Use **spaced repetition** from Day 1

- Create **a 30-60-90 revision plan**

- Weekly review using **flashcards + mind maps**

Reminder: Real retention builds in small doses over time, not in a week-long cramming session.

****

9.5 Mistake #4: Passive Reading Without Recall

The Problem:

Reading and underlining without testing yourself.

Why It Fails:

- Gives a false sense of confidence

- Fails in actual MCQs

- No mental retrieval practice

Fix It:

- Use the **blurting method** (write everything you remember from a topic)

- Make **5 MCQs or recall questions** after each chapter

- Explain concepts to a study buddy or a mirror

Learning = Output. Always test yourself after input.

****

9.6 Mistake #5: Memorizing Without Visual Anchors

The Problem:

Trying to remember long definitions, lists, and cycles as raw text.

Why It Fails:

- The brain forgets plain text fast

- No emotional or visual hook

Fix It:

- Use **sketches, metaphors, and analogies**

- Turn concepts into **cartoons or comic scenes**

- Link lists to the **memory palace locations**

Example: Imagine hormones like tiny messengers flying through a post office (endocrine system) with special delivery labels.

****

9.7 Mistake #6: Studying Everything Equally

The Problem:

Spending equal time on all chapters—even the ones with fewer NEET weightage.

Why It Fails:

- Wastes time

- Reduces time for high-yield chapters

Fix It:

- Use **NEET question analysis** to identify the most tested topics

- Prioritize **Human Physiology, Genetics, Plant Physiology, and Ecology**

- Revise **high-weightage chapters** more often with visuals and tests

****

9.8 Mistake #7: Overloading the Brain

The Problem:

Trying to cover too many topics in a single sitting.

Why It Fails:

- Low retention

- Mental fatigue

- Confused recall

Fix It:

- Follow the **Pomodoro Technique** (25 mins study + 5 min break)

- Study Chapter 1 **deeply** rather than three shallowly

- Use **focused visual rituals**: Sketch → Recall → Quiz

****

9.9 Mistake #8: Studying Without a System

The Problem:

No plan, no tracking, no method—just random effort.

Why It Fails:

- Inconsistent progress

- Forgetting what was studied

- No direction in revision

Fix It:

- Use a **Visual Study Planner**

- Track progress with a **daily ritual checklist**

- Apply the **"Visual Learning Loop"**:

  1. Study with visuals

  2. Recall actively

  3. Sketch or map

  4. Revise weekly

5. Test with MCQs

****

9.10 Final Thoughts: Mistakes Are Teachers

It's okay to make mistakes—what matters is **correcting them fast**. With every mistake you avoid, you get:

- Better clarity

- Faster revision

- Higher confidence

- Stronger retention

This chapter is your shortcut to avoiding years of trial and error.

"It's not just about what you study—it's about *how you study it that makes all the difference.*"

Get ready for the final chapter, where you'll put everything together into a **personalized, flexible NEET Biology Mastery Plan**!

Chapter 10: Your Personalized Bio-Mastery Plan

10.1 You're Not Just a Student — You're a Strategy Designer

You now have powerful tools:

- Mind maps

- Mnemonics

- Sketching

- Memory palaces

- Active recall

- Spaced repetition

- Daily rituals

- Visual planning

But real mastery happens when you **turn tools into a system**, customized to how *you* think, learn, and revise.

This chapter helps you build your **own flexible, goal-driven NEET Biology prep system** — one that grows with you, adapts to your pace, and keeps you *mentally strong* all the way to exam day.

****

10.2 Step 1: Know Your Strengths and Gaps

Before building your plan, you must first **diagnose** your current standing.

Self-Assessment:

Create a table like this and rate each unit (1–5):

Chapter/Unit	Understanding	Recall	Diagram Accuracy
Human Physiology	4	3	2
Plant Physiology	2	2	1
Genetics	3	2	3

This helps you focus **more time on weak zones** and visually **reinforce strengths**.

****

10.3 Step 2: Set Your Bio-Mastery Goals

Set **clear, visual goals** — not just "study more."

Examples:

- "Revise all NCERT diagrams 4 times before NEET."

- "Create one mind map every day."

- "Master 50 mnemonics for high-yield topics"

- "Solve 1000 Biology MCQs using visual recall only."

Stick these goals on your wall or planner as *reminders and motivators.*

****

10.4 Step 3: Build Your Weekly Visual Study Plan

Here's a sample framework:

Day	Task
Monday	New topic with sketching + 5 MCQs
Tuesday	Revise the previous mind map + memory palace.
Wednesday	Practice diagram from memory

Thursday	Active recall + quiz yourself
Friday	Create mnemonics + share with a friend.
Saturday	Solve 30 MCQs from weak topics.
Sunday	Review 3 topics + reflect in journal.

Create your plan using this model, and **adjust it based on your syllabus progress.**

****

10.5 Step 4: Organize Your Bio Toolkit

Set up these folders (physical or digital):

- **Mind Map Master Folder** — one for each NCERT chapter

- **Diagram Sketchbook** — draw & label all key visuals

- **Mnemonic Wall** — paste or list all creative memory aids

- **Flashcard Deck** — Anki, Notion, or handmade

- **Mistake Tracker** — wrong answers + corrections + fix

This becomes your **ultimate NEET Biology revision kit.**

10.6 Step 5: Track Your Progress Visually

Make learning *visible* and rewarding:

- Use sticker charts or trackers

- Tick off completed chapters

- Highlight "strong" and "weak" zones weekly

- Color-code chapters:

    o Green = Mastered

    o Yellow = Needs Review

    o Red = Needs Reinforcement

This adds **emotional motivation** and helps avoid overwhelm.

****

10.7 Step 6: Protect Your Mindset

Biology prep isn't just academic—it's emotional and mental.

Here's how to **keep your confidence strong**:

- **Rituals over randomness** — follow your routine even on low-energy days

- **Celebrate small wins** — finished a diagram? High-five yourself!

- **Avoid comparison** — your journey is unique

- **Trust your system** — you've built a powerful toolkit; now *use it daily*

- **Take breaks** — creativity flows when your brain rests

****

10.8 Sample Student Bio-Mastery Planner (Visual)

Week	Topics	Visual Task	MCQs	Score
1	Plant Growth	Sketch + Mnemonic	20	16
2	Digestion	Diagram recall + Flashcards	30	26
3	Genetics	Memory Palace + Mind Map	25	20

Students can track their performance visually and see improvement over time.

****

10.9 Bonus: The Night Before NEET

What to do the night before the exam?

- No cramming

- Review only **mind maps, mnemonics, and diagrams**

- Take a quick walk through your **memory palace**

- Visualize success and stay calm

- Sleep well — it's part of your memory system!

****

10.10 Final Words: You're Ready

You're no longer studying Biology the old way.

You've now built a *brain-smart system* designed for visual memory, confidence, clarity, and NEET-level precision.

This isn't just a book. It's a **toolkit, coach, planner, and mindset mentor.**

Use it every day, revise strategically, and walk into the exam **fully prepared and mentally empowered.**

"You don't rise to the level of your motivation. You fall to the level of your systems. Now you have a system — make it unstoppable."

****

Wrap-Up Checklist: Your Biology Mastery System

- Created mind maps for all key topics

- Made and memorized at least 30 mnemonics

- Practiced all the NCERT diagrams from memory

- Built 3+ memory palaces for long chapters

- Solved 1000+ MCQs using recall strategies

- Used a spaced repetition planner for 60+ days

- Confidently explain any chapter from a sketch

If these are ticked, **you're NEET Biology-ready.**

Bonus Chapter 11: How to Retain Biology in Long-Term Memory

The Brain-Science Secrets to Never Forgetting What You Learn

11.1 Why You Forget — Even After Studying So Hard

NEET aspirants often say,

"I studied this chapter last month... but I've forgotten everything!"

That's because they're storing content in **short-term memory** with no system for **long-term consolidation**.

Here's the truth:

Your brain *doesn't keep* what you *don't revisit, recall, and emotionally connect with*.

****

11.2 How Long-Term Memory Works (in Simple Words)

Your brain remembers best when:

- It sees **patterns**

- It gets **emotionally involved** (even fun mnemonics count!)

- It's asked to **recall**, not just re-read

- It receives **spaced, progressive exposure**

****

11.3 Tools That Convert Short-Term to Long-Term Memory

Tool	How It Helps
Spaced Repetition	Tells your brain, "This is important."
Sketching from Memory	Builds visual + motor memory
Teaching Others	Reinforces ideas through reprocessing
Mind Maps	Connects ideas across chapters
Memory Palaces	Uses spatial and emotional memory cues

11.4 Practical System to Retain Biology for NEET

The "4R Cycle":

1. **Read** – Understand using visual tools

2. **Recall** – Without looking, write or draw from memory

3. **Reinforce** – Add mnemonics, diagrams, and quiz questions

4. **Repeat** – Schedule smart revision (1–3–7–14–30 days)

****

11.5 NEET Revision Planner: What to Do After Studying a Chapter

Day	Task
Day 1	Mind map + blurting method
Day 3	Flashcards or a memory test
Day 7	Teach a friend or a mirror.
Day 14	MCQs + diagram recall
Day 30	Final summary + visual walkthrough

11.6 Final Thought

"Learning is remembering. And remembering is revisiting—smartly, visually, and emotionally."

If you use the tools in this chapter with intention, **you won't just study Biology — you'll own it.**

Bonus Chapter 12: NEET Biology Exam Strategy – Smart Recall Under Pressure

How to Stay Calm, Think Fast, and Solve More Questions with Confidence

12.1 The Real Exam Problem Isn't Just Memory — It's Retrieval Speed

You might *know* the answer, but in the exam hall...

- You panic

- You blank out

- You can't recall fast enough

That's not a memory problem — it's a **retrieval problem under stress.**

This chapter teaches you to train your brain to **recall information faster, even under pressure**, with greater clarity.

****

12.2 Shift from "Studying Mode" to "Exam Mode"

To perform well, you must practice simulating **the exam environment.**

Strategy	Benefit
Timed MCQ Sets (30 min – 45 Qs)	Boosts speed and focus
Mental Visualization Practice	Helps recall diagrams and mnemonics fast
Rapid Recall Sessions	Speak out answers quickly in short bursts.
Anchor Mnemonics	Use triggers for fast information access.

12.3 How to Use Visual Tools in the Exam

- Before the test, mentally **walk through your Memory Palaces**

- Use mnemonics as **anchors** to trigger connected concepts

- **Visualize** diagrams when solving clinical or application-based questions

- Use **mental flowcharts** to eliminate wrong options in tricky MCQs

****

12.4 "Mind Under Pressure" Rituals

Use these in the exam hall to calm and reset:

- Take three deep breaths

- Recall your strongest topic first

- Visualize a success anchor (e.g., your top-scoring test memory)

- Begin with easy questions to build momentum

****

12.5 The NEET Biology Exam Sprint Plan

Time Window	What to Do
First 20 min	Solve all easy/familiar questions
Next 30 min	Tackle moderate-level ones using visual recall.
Last 20 min	Revisit diagrams & tricky options; avoid overthinking.

12.6 Final Words

"NEET is not just a test of memory. It's a test of recall, under pressure, with precision."

This chapter helps you make **your brain exam-ready, not just content-ready.**

May I Ask You For A Small Favor?

First, I want to thank you for reading this book. You could have chosen any other book, but you took mine, and I appreciate this. I hope you have at least a few actionable insights that will positively impact your daily life.

Can I ask for 30 seconds more of your time?

I'd love it if you could leave a review of the book. That will help me grow my readership by encouraging folks to take a chance on my books.

Keeping it straight - reviews are the lifeblood of any author.

It will take less than a minute of your time but will tremendously help me reach out to more people.

If you liked this book, please consider posting an honest review on your preferred retailer. And I'd love to see your review. Thanks for your support.

Join Me

Learn and practice all the techniques from this book by joining my program.

Click **here** or scan the QR code below:

Thank You!

9 7 9 8 8 9 9 6 1 9 3 3 5